Unveiling The Mask of The Pretender

Lamonte Faison

Email: lamontefaison@aol.com
www.lfaison.com

Published by
L.D. Faison International
Copyright © 2009 by L.D. Faison

Manufactured in the United States of America

ISBN 0-9765071-2-9
EAN 13 : 978-0976507123

To order additional copies, please contact us.
BookSurge
www.booksurge.com
1-866-308-6235
orders@booksurge.com

dedication: This book is dedicated to all of the people who are looking to find their way. Understand that true freedom comes when we release the junk that is in our system: hatred, bitterness, self-pity and the myriad of excuses that we use on a daily basis. Special thanks to Allison Hampton who put up with me during my time of indecisiveness and Katina Fields who allows me to be myself without judgment. To all of the folks who want to be free—it's already done, you are just not aware. Accept it and move on into your destiny.

Table of Contents

prologue: Light passes through with clarity.

It allows you to see who you are if you let it. I have failed.

Putting up walls preventing the light from passing through, which prohibits me from seeing who I am.

The question is this: Do I really want to see myself or do I want to continue to hide behind the mask and evade the truth?

The world is over-saturated with pretenders, and I've pretended for a long time. I've pretended in my school days, as well as my adulthood. I've seduced women in the church and deceived them. I've hung out with Bitterness and become best friends with Anger, and somehow I am related to Manipulation. And let's not forget that I am Deception's half-cousin.

I'm too proud to seek counseling; after all, I am a minister. Keeping my secrets bottled up, I don't want to reveal what I am, or at least what I'm battling. My image needs to be protected so it's covered up like a body in a burial grave. My need for attention is unbearable and I'm seeking it and acting out every day to get it. I'm too embarrassed to tell someone that I have a problem. Meanwhile, the family suffers, the members suffer and I'm suffering.

Even at this present moment, I'm battling the spirit of lust and the fear of being alone and nobody knows it but me. What will you do with this information? Will you now examine yourself and your ways? Or will you continue down the path of being like me…

A PRETENDER

Chapter 1
MY PREY

I preyed on women in the church. I was an addict, and their vulnerability was my drug of choice. I would seek them out like a Lion stalking its prey. This was easy because I was a single minister. The opportunity to have one-on-one sessions with these precious women would arise often. I used the office of a minister to lure the women in; not that I wasn't called to minister, but I perverted my ministry, and allowed the enemy to lead me, instead of allowing God to guide me. Women would come to the altar for prayer. They would discuss their issues with me, and that's when the games would begin. The goal—Sex.

When a woman stood in my line for prayer, I was already scoping her out to see if she was my type, while simultaneously plotting to get her naked. Some women would approach me, and I would literally feel them out. I would hold their hand, paying close attention to how they held mine, and I could instinctively tell when they wanted me to caress them or to seek them out later. I even had a young lady come up and wink at me, and the last thing a guy like me needs is a woman winking at him. That's like teasing the rat with cheese, and, of course, we all know the rat cannot resist. I ate the cheese and then asked for more. I know that's crazy, but it's real—I couldn't help myself.

Where the issue of lust is concerned, I should have sat myself down a long time ago, but I have seen so many ministers be promiscuous and still preach, so I felt that I could do the same thing. Why should I be any different? I covered up my weakness for the ladies and wore the mask for so long that I invited the devil in for dinner and he never left.

I have always been weak when it comes to the female species. Just the sight of them—their beauty and their smiles—was enough to get me aroused. I wanted to please them. I wanted to see the expression on their faces when I had brought them to that point of climax. I got off on that, but it wasn't just any woman, she had to be gorgeous in my eyes.

Most of the women I preyed on found me equally as attractive, and often times, they were more than just a little flirtatious. In a sense, they were playing a game too, but I'm sure they thought I would never call their bluff. By the time they finally realized that the game they were playing was my invention, it was already too late. I had won, claimed my prize, and was ready to move on. But there were a few that didn't plan to sleep with me. Somehow, I impressed or charmed them to the point that they let down their guard. I used every slick word in the book to find their vulnerable spot. I was good at putting words together, and I used that to my advantage.

After I prayed with these women, I would get their phone numbers, one way or the other, and start the dialogue that would lead to their inevitable surrender. Once I sensed that they were comfortable with me, I would engage in a different type of talk. I would no longer talk about church stuff, but about things in the world and our place and purpose in it. Then I would slowly coax them into accepting an invitation onto my turf. Nothing too dramatic, of course—just a simple invite to the movies or dinner, or the ever-popular, Bible study. Before they could answer, I would encourage them to invite their friends along. "Maybe we can play some cards or dominoes or something," I'd say. The goal was to make her feel as comfortable as possible, and telling her that she didn't have to come alone alleviated any hesitation she may have felt being solely in my company. Once that bridge was crossed, the guard would come down and that was when I went for it, because at that point, I had her trust. So much trust, in fact, that she usually elected not to bring her friends. I became a pillow for her to lay on, a fixture in her comfort zone. I would ask her if she was hungry. I did all I could to make her feel cozy and safe—all the while, luring her in, deeper and deeper. I knew that once I got her there, it was almost guaranteed that I would sleep with her, even if it didn't happen that night. I learned early on that women loved for men to romance them, care for them, and love them. They wanted someone to listen to them and that's just what I did. I pretended to care.

Some of the signs of vulnerability that I looked for with these women was their need to discuss their past, or even present relationships. Most of the time, these women wouldn't have anything good to say when it came to their exes or spouses. One of the complaints I would often hear from a woman was that her significant other wasn't intimate with her—he didn't spend time with her. Regardless of my true opinion, I would agree with everything they said. Whatever he didn't do, I would do. If he didn't buy flowers, I'd buy them, even if it was only a single rose. They didn't need a dozen—they just needed the gesture.

My objective was to show the women that I was different: kind, patient, a good listener and charming—all of the things that I wasn't, but pretended to be. These women just wanted to be told that they were beautiful, and I accommodated them. I told them whatever they wanted to hear, and it worked. The game was in full throttle and I kept getting better and better. The field of vulnerability worked so well that I adopted the strategy of telling people what they wanted to hear just to get over

Chapter 2
LUST IN THE WORKPLACE

I used the same strategy with women at my work-place to get into their pants. I've seduced and manip-ulated women; married, single, divorced—it didn't matter. One thing that I've learned on this journey is that women love men who are in positions of power. It could be an ice cream truck—if you own it, they're on you. I recall several situations at my job as an instruc-tor in which women would make comments to me about my looks, my confidence, my walk—and I loved it! Most men that I know love this kind of attention, so why should I be any different? During this same time, there was a rumor going around that I was a dog and that I was trying to sleep with all of the women attend-ing my class, but despite all the information-sharing going on amongst these women, they slept with me anyway. Evidently, the fact that they had heard that I was no good was not a deterrent.

There was a particular young lady who I had already seen once before. I knew that she was sched-uled to attend my class so I waited with anticipation for her to arrive. When she entered the room, I spoke to her, but she paid me no attention. After class, I saw her on the highway going home. I pulled up next to her and asked her to pull over to the side of the road. I invited her out for coffee and she accepted. Although she had paid me no real attention earlier in the evening, I knew that she had been told some things about me, and that she was trying hard not to give in. Instead of avoiding the issue, I addressed it head-on. I asked her what she had heard about me. She told me that some of the other women enrolled in my classes had told her to watch out for me—that I was going to try to talk to her because she was pretty. "Why did you stop on the highway if you had heard that?" I asked, to which she replied, "There's something about you."

Unbeknownst to her, the initial seduction had begun long before she became a willing participant. It started in class when I called on her to answer questions and made little comments to spark her interest. I maintained a professional demeanor and never wavered from my instruction, knowing all along that it was intriguing to her. Every time I looked her way, she would look in another direction—that's when I knew I had her. This was the game I played. I played with her emotions a little—told her how pretty she was and how much I admired her for stepping up to be the best officer she could be. Basically, I stroked her ego into overdrive. By the end of that day, I had her phone number. A week later, we were having sex in my car.

I met another woman at work who was also very pretty. I'd had my eye on her for some time. We flirted back and forth; every time I saw her, she would smile at me, and I would smile back. I wanted to sleep with this girl so badly that I could smell her even when she wasn't in the room—I could almost taste her. I knew she wanted me, but I was reluctant to approach her for fear of being hit with a sexual harassment accusation. So I waited until we were outside of the workplace. I soon learned that she was married, but that didn't matter to me. One day, we went to a company gathering at a bar, and we talked and played pool. At the end of the night, we exchanged phone numbers. I was comfortable with the situation because we were outside of work, and I could say pretty much anything that I wanted—and I did. I told her to give me a call after she left the bar, that maybe we could go somewhere and talk.

I can assure you that talking was not part of my plan. Eventually she did call, and we made arrangements to meet at a park. When she arrived, I played the strong silent type and encouraged her to do most of the talking—I wanted her to think that I was a good listener. She talked about her husband and the things he did that troubled her, how he didn't please her anymore, or pay her any attention, and, of course, I said I was sorry to hear that, and all of the things that I was supposed to say—everything she wanted to hear. I just wanted to console her and be there for her while she was going through this difficult time. When the consoling was all over, I got what I wanted. She turned out to be someone that I could've been with in a relationship, possibly even married. But that wasn't going to happen since both of us were already married.

Nevertheless, we made passionate love in the park that night. The chemistry was magnetic—I didn't want it to end. We even hooked up at work in the parking lot—I couldn't get enough of her. She told me that when she took showers, she thought about me and touched herself. She knew what to say and do to keep me excited!

One day, the fun ended. I guess she started feeling guilty. She told me that she had confessed to her priest about our affair, and even worse, she told him my name. I was beside myself. I couldn't comprehend why she would tell another man about me, albeit a priest, and take the chance of exposing our affair. That was the pretender talking. A pretender doesn't want to be discovered, so to have my identity revealed was a real setback for me. Sadly, it was over, and I haven't heard from her since. The guilt was too much for her, and I truly understood. I had been selfish, and thought only of how I might be hurt, or how my game might suffer if word got out. The truth is, the women were already talking. Any reputation I was trying to protect had already been dissected and destroyed, but I still had my ego to contend with and my ego didn't want my name out there any more than it already was.

Countless events like this one occurred on a consistent basis. I was possessed with this power. Sexual dominance gave me the confidence that I was somebody; it felt good, but also bad in a strange way. I guess somewhere deep down inside, I knew that the women were going to get hurt by my actions, lies and manipulation, and I'm not sure that I really wanted that to happen, but I did not, or perhaps, could not, stop. The games just continued—and I kept on pretending.

Chapter 3
A FRIEND INDEED

I had a friend who had a peculiar habit of dropping his fiancée off at my house whenever he was angry with her, because he knew that I would offer her a ride home. He did this quite often, and because I was his friend, he trusted me. Little did he know that I was falling for her, or, at least, lusting after her. During these episodes of abandonment, she and I talked about their issues, and I became her sounding board. She was a beautiful young lady, so it wasn't hard for me to pay attention and listen to her. One day, he dropped her off at my house, and she and I began to chat as usual, but this night was different—this night, I didn't take her home. I asked her if she wanted to stay the night, because I was tired and didn't feel up to driving across town. Whether or not that was the truth, she had no problem staying.

I asked her if she would sleep in my bed. I didn't want her to sleep on the couch, and I didn't want to sleep on the couch, so I opened up my bed to her. We talked for most of the night, and I listened intently and fed her head with "sweet nothings"—literally. To accelerate the inevitable, I started a conversation about her fiancée leaving her at my house. I told her that if he cared about her, he would've taken her home himself. The more I talked about him, the angrier she got, but I didn't care because I wanted to be with her that night. And I did, with no remorse. I'm sure she slept with me just to get back at him, but I didn't care—I got what I wanted and apparently she got what she needed because we continued to sleep together after that on a regular basis. I would go to her house, hang out, and then we would have sex. Sometimes I would arrive just moments after he had left.

After she and her boyfriend (my friend) broke up, she told him that I tried to come on to her, which completely threw me for a loop. I couldn't understand why she told him such a lie, or better yet, why she told him anything at all. I guess she was avoiding her own truth, not wanting to reveal who she was and what she was battling. Of course, I understood what she was experiencing—pretenders always understand other pretenders. She was feeling guilty, and probably thought that I would tell someone so she wanted to get her version of the events on record to reduce my credibility. Whatever the case, she was in a state of denial about her own proclivities. To sum it up in one word, she was *pretending*—covering up her own issues, shifting the blame onto me and wearing the mask that many of us wear.

Why would a man drop his girlfriend off at another man's house for him to take her home anyway? I've always been baffled by his behavior, and although I don't know what was going through his head, I do know that he was an accomplice in helping me to attain a goal that, in all honesty, I probably would have pursued with or without his efforts. If you think I'm a dog, that would be accurate, because a dog doesn't care where it lays or what other dog it mates with—and neither did I. During those rare moments of repentance, I would re-analyze the circumstances leading up to that episode and justify my actions by blaming him. I would tell myself: *He knew my weakness. He should never have put me in that position. Why did he drop her off at my place? If he hadn't dropped her off I wouldn't have slept with her.* But my regrets would soon be replaced with the acceptance of the truth. If it hadn't happened with her, it would've happened with someone else, because I was driven by my desires and like any willing passenger, I was just along for the ride. I've slept with countless girlfriends, fiancé's and wives—pleasure seekers know no guilt.

Chapter 4
THE WONDER YEARS

For as long as I can remember, I've exhibited this type of behavior. I am to blame, no one else. It's despicable, and a disgrace for me to operate the way that I have—to treat women the way that I have. I won't make any excuses. I've spent a lot of time reminiscing about my past, trying to figure out why I have been so promiscuous and deceiving.

I remember an incident that happened when I was nine years old. My family and I were visiting relatives out of town, and all of the men were in the living room watching television, drinking and having a good time. Being curious, I wanted to see what was going on, so I walked out of the bedroom and into the living room and was pleasantly surprised to find them huddled around the television watching a porno flick. The sight of naked women got me excited, and I wanted to see more. At that age, I was impressionable. Hell—at my age today, I'm impressionable. Shortly thereafter, I began to experiment. I would get on top of stuffed animals and perform perverted acts. I was only acting out what I had seen. In my eyes, this was harmless behavior, but as I got older, my curiosity took on a life of its own.

There was a time where I would sneak into my stepfather's room and watch porn on cable, and masturbate. My favorite pastimes became grabbing girls' butts, and masturbating with a girl or a porno. I would run around the school looking for pretty girls and literally grab their butts while fantasizing about sleeping with them

This continued well into my junior high and high school days. Probably the most prominent memory I had was when I was about 12 years old. There were some girls that lived across the street from my family. The girls were beautiful, and I wanted to see them naked. They were flirtatious with me, which only made me more determined and anxious to make it happen. One of the girls had a see-through curtain on her bedroom window. One day, while she was getting undressed, I ran across the street and looked into her window to watch her. It was so exciting my heart was beating fast from the anticipation of seeing her flesh. It felt like I was having sex with her. There I was, a 12-year-old peeping tom at night, acting as an average teenager by day.

A few years later, my parents moved into an apartment. I was walking in the complex when I saw a pretty woman through her window. I got excited like I did the first time, and immediately hid behind the tree to watch her. She looked so good that I just wanted to knock on her window to let her know that I was watching. Somehow, I thought that she might actually like the fact that someone was watching her. But that fantasy would soon be over. After a few moments, a large male figure walked into the room. He was about six-feet-two and 220 pounds, and that ruined it for me. I left thinking that I was out of control. I started thinking about what could happen to me if I ever got caught. I had heard stories of people who have gotten shot for doing the same thing that I was doing. And, of course, there was the possibility of getting arrested. But I was hooked. It seemed like I enjoyed the adventure. The excitement, the anxiety—it was great, but I cried every night, because inside, my soul was dark. Still, I kept right on doing what I was doing, but when I was around other people, I would act like everything was great. I assure you, life was far from great.

This runaway train of a life was out of control, but I was too ashamed to talk about it with my mother and father. My parents and I weren't close, so going to them and opening up about my behavior wasn't an option. My stepfather and I didn't get along at all and the fact that I didn't know he was my "step"father at the time only added to my confusion and inner turmoil. My mother and I had a decent relationship, but confiding in her meant having to endure her preaching, and I was *never* in the mood for that. Furthermore, I didn't want to be looked upon as a pervert or a freak, especially because I felt like a freak, so it was safer for me to internalize it. Sometimes I thought about men who raped women and the motivation behind their actions. Were they lonely? Did they do it because they were unable to get sex on their own? What would make a man want to do that to a woman? I needed to understand them so that I could clearly identify the distinction between me and them. I needed to know I wasn't like them. I hoped and prayed daily that I wasn't like them.

I saw how Catholic priests would put little boys through hell because of their inclinations, but they were at the mercy of their own shame so they never sought help. I didn't consider what I did to be a violation, even though I was invading the privacy of women I didn't know. How long would I keep taking these risks? There were moments when I think I wanted to get caught—that it would be easier if it were all out in the open, easier to just deal with the shame. But my behavior was compulsive, triggered by a thought, a smell, a memory, a beautiful smile inviting me to want to know her, conquer her. All of it took me back to the root of my addiction—back to who I really was—a pretender. I was two men living in one body; wearing the masks of different personalities. There was the external part of me, the Oscar-worthy actor who had mastered the art of my strategy. Then there was the other man: frustrated, confused, and at times, afraid, struggling with issues so deep that my soul bears the scars to this day. But through it all, the mask remained, and I traveled the road of Pretend all the way into adulthood, the Church and my marriages.

Chapter 5
MARRIAGE NUMBER 1

As many of us do, I was looking for an outlet. I figured if I found myself a wife, then everything would be fine—no more sleeping around, no more manipulating. So I married a young lady who was old-fashioned, a few years older than I was and a lot more mature. By nature, I was always a show-off. I liked attention and I liked to be seen. Ours was not a match of compatibility, and the marriage proved to be a mistake on both of our parts.

The tide caught up with me quickly. I wasn't spending any time with my wife, not even making love to her. The time that we did spend together in the bedroom brought her no real satisfaction. I didn't engage her. All I wanted to do was to watch her masturbate. She was reluctant because she wanted to be held, not treated like some whore. I would get angry when she didn't want to do what I asked. I would blame her for my dissatisfaction, and tell her that she was too conservative and even though I didn't want to hold her, I expected to be held when it was all over. It was selfish on my part, but at the time, I didn't see it that way. I figured that I was the man, she was my wife, and regardless of her feelings or desires, she was supposed to honor what I wanted. It wasn't about intimacy for me. It was strictly about pleasure. I wanted to see her face when she climaxed, and that's it. When I was done masturbating, it was over. No feelings. No remorse. Nothing.

In hindsight, I ask myself, "How could I have been so selfish as to bring another soul into my chaos?" She didn't deserve the pain that I caused her. She gave of herself completely—I gave a fraction of that. I pretended to be in love, when I had no idea what love was. To make matters worse, I didn't just bring her into my madness, but her son also. I was arrogant and more interested in showing off for my friends, than in showing up for my wife and stepson. This woman owned a house, had two cars and, by all outward appearances, had her life together. Yet, I was a grown man who didn't have a pot to pee in, but I had enough ego to play Mr. Big Shot, bragging to my friends daily about what I owned, when in fact, I didn't own anything. I was just a nobody, perfectly content to live off of my wife's hard work.

We sought counseling with our pastor and his wife—our attempt to make one last go of it. They were great, but by then, the demands that my wife and I had put on one another were too unrealistic. The strain on our relationship and the dishonesty that had taken up residence in our marriage made it impossible to go on. I wasn't even honest with the pastor, defeating any possibility of us getting on the right track. The first rule of thumb when going to counseling is to be honest so that you can try to work on those issues that are prohibiting your relationship from flourishing. I did not possess all the ingredients needed for a healthy union. I lacked honesty and integrity. I perpetrated a fraud, knowing that I wasn't ready for a relationship. But, I convinced her when she was my bride-to-be that I was her dream man, only to smash her dreams shortly thereafter. *To that lady, I apologize to you for being self-centered, dishonest and controlling. May God heal you from the pain that I have caused.* Our marriage lasted a year, but we were physically separated after six months.

Chapter 6
CYBER AFFAIRS

While married, I would spend at least five hours a day on my days off, chatting on the Internet and romancing a certain lady, while my wife was in the other room. Sometimes, she would walk in and immediately, I would panic and close the screen. To this day, I'm not sure if she knew that I was cheating on her, or even if she knows that I traveled to Oakland, California, to spend the weekend with this young lady.

That's right. This woman, whom I had chatted with for only a month, paid for a plane ticket for me to come see her, and of course, I obliged her. At the time, I told my wife that I was going to visit family. In reality, I was romancing in a hotel with this other woman, having sex, walking on the beach, eating like a king and having a good time. Meanwhile, her husband was off on a business trip—or, at least, that's what he told her. She even took me by her home, and said that we could stay there for a night, but, of course, I declined that invitation. I knew better than that.

The fact of the matter was that I was being pleased by someone else. She was willing to do anything for me, but there were no ties. I felt no pressure or obligation to her. It was exciting and easy, so I enjoyed it. She shared with me the fact that her husband did not hold her or spend time with her, which made me question whether he was really on a business trip or if he was off doing the same thing that I was doing with his wife. Nevertheless, I pretended with her just as I had in my marriage. The sad truth was that neither relationship was going to work.

Chapter 7
MARRIAGE NUMBER 2

After all the destruction and the pain that I have caused, after all the tears and the apologies, you would think I that I would've learned my lesson, but as the saying goes, "a hard head makes a soft behind". I indulged, again, in another marriage. If you're counting, this was marriage number two. This time, I married a beautiful young lady who was a few years younger than I was. She was well-educated, spoke two languages, and held a degree from a prestigious college. She was a great, loving woman. Who could ask for more? But with no real counseling, mentoring and no direction, I couldn't really expect the marriage to be successful.

The pastor that was counseling us was known to be controlling and verbally abusive to his own wife, so I didn't get much out of those counseling sessions. I was too busy judging his actions. I could've sought more counseling if I had wanted to. I do realize it was my responsibility to do so and I chose not to. I believe that I rushed into this marriage, partly because I wanted to have sex, and I couldn't wait any longer. In the church, all I ever hear from my pastor is, "It is better to marry than to burn". Since we had agreed not to have sex until we were married and I didn't want to "burn", I was ready to get this thing on the road. Six months after we met, I thought I was ready to be a husband.

I felt good about myself to a certain extent. I had learned a lot, matured in a lot of ways, so I went in with good intentions. We married on December 4, 1999, three years after my first marriage, but I soon found that good intentions do not make up for a lack of direction or therapy. I was still dealing with, or rather avoiding, the hurt and pain of my first marriage, because I had really wanted it to work and it didn't. Then there was the fact that I had bragged to all my friends about how good I had it, only to have to face the embarrassment of losing it all. But, instead of getting help, I just kept it bottled up inside me until now. But suffice it to say, I continued to wear the mask of a pretender, convincing myself that I was okay and I could handle everything.

In the midst of all of this, I was still a minister in the church. Six months into this marriage, I committed adultery once again—this time with a woman at my new place of work. What a fiasco! We talked for awhile. I got to know her a little bit, and eventually, I felt comfortable enough to take her to buy some cigarettes. We flirted with each other, and after a while we made plans to meet at her apartment. I was supposed to be a security officer for the place where she was staying, so I should have been busy watching out for her and the other residents that lived there. The only thing that I was watching was her naked body. We had sex in her bedroom, and afterward, I got up and went back to work like nothing ever happened. Later on that night, the young lady approached me and asked what I was doing the next day. I told her I was going to hang out with my wife. Oops—did I forget to mention my wife? She was shocked that I was married.

The very next day, the unthinkable happened. I received a call from a lieutenant with the Metro Police Department, stating that I needed to come in for questioning regarding allegations that I had raped this woman. What a blow! That was so far from the truth. Shortly after that, I received a call from my boss, advising me my services were no longer needed. It is at that time that I tried to tell the boss that I didn't sleep with the young lady, and I most assuredly didn't rape her. Apparently, he believed me and gave me the benefit of the doubt. The unfortunate thing about this incident is that I was lying about not sleeping with her to my employer, in an effort to save my job. My credibility and integrity were on the line. The fact that I was lying was bound to come out. And shortly thereafter, it did.

Once I completed my interview with the police, wherein I was completely truthful, I was informed that the police would be contacting my employer regarding the incident.

To this day, I never called the boss back, too embarrassed to face him. My credibility and integrity were shot. And I still had a major hurdle to cross—how would I explain this to my wife?

After arriving at home and pacing the floor for a couple of hours, my wife finally arrived. It wasn't long before she realized that something was wrong. I told her that some girl on my job accused me of raping her, and of course that wasn't true, but I also told her that I didn't sleep with the girl. I pondered telling her the truth, because in the back of my mind, I knew that I was going to get a call from the police again. So I broke down and told her that I slept with the woman. I began crying, telling her that I was sorry for lying to her, and for hurting her. But I reassured her that I didn't rape anyone. She started crying and I told her that I would leave if she wanted me to. I also informed her that I had to go down for questioning and asked if she would go with me for support. How inconsiderate on my part! I had already humiliated my wife and embarrassed myself, and then had the audacity to ask her to support me. This was the same woman that I tried to control, got mad at, even belittled at times, but she was still willing to be in my corner. By this time, I was stressed out, hurting and contemplating suicide. I cried, and then cried again, thinking I was going to jail. I was scared sick—the thought of going to prison for a crime I didn't commit, but at the same time knowing that I put myself in that situation.

Once again, I made God my best friend—you know how we call on God when we are in trouble. One thing about God is it doesn't matter how many different faces you put on, He knows the real you, so there was no need for me to lie to God—I just wanted His help, and boy, I needed it fast! My world was turned upside down. It seemed like all of the dirt I'd done in the past was coming back to haunt me. On the flip-side of that, I was thinking that if He didn't help me I would completely understand, knowing how many times I have let Him down by making promises that I couldn't keep or didn't keep. *Lord, I apologize to you also for not being the son that You called me to be. I'm sorry for crucifying You once again on the cross. I need you to help me be better—I can't do this on my own. I need You. God, I'm not going to make any promises—I'm just going to repent. I ask You to keep me strong, to lead and guide me.*

Just as always, God came through. No charges were filed, and I was free again—from the law, but not from my troubles. I was still incarcerated in my mind by this addiction. I needed to figure out how to over-come this obstacle.

My relationship with my wife became real rocky. She had lost trust in me. I continued to try to tell her that I was going to change, but as you know, talk is cheap. I continued to cheat on her. A lot of times, she didn't even know it—at least I don't think she knew. But I knew. I also knew that I was dying softly, and that I needed to get this lust demon out of me and under control. One day, my wife called me to say that she was not coming home for a few days. I was sick about it, but I understood. The fact that I disrespected her and myself was a tragedy in itself. Eventually, she came home, after days of us communicating by phone only. One of the conditions for her coming home was to enroll both of us in counseling, which I agreed to. At that time, I would do anything to keep my baby—I loved her, and still do, to this day. So, I agreed.

Chapter 8
MARRIAGE COUNSELING

My wife and I did go to counseling, but I manip-ulated it. I did all of the talking. I told the counselor that I did all these things, and that everything was my fault. I agreed with the counselor on every topic, as if to say, "I got this. I know it all, and you, Sir, with your Master's degree, don't know nearly as much as I do." I was arrogant—so arrogant that I couldn't even stand myself. Needless to say, I didn't learn much from that session. My wife even bought books to help us, but I never made time to read them. And my marriage suf-fered because of it.

Later on, we decided to move out of state together so she could be closer to her family. Upon arriving to our new state, I was hit with a major blow. I found out that my wife was cheating on me, as well. Her cell phone rang one day while she was in the shower. It kept ringing, so I picked it up, thinking it was her mom or some other family member. It went to text, so I checked the message, and it was a guy telling my wife how he wanted to do different things to her, and that he couldn't wait to see her again. I wasn't as angry as you might think—shocked, yes, but not angry. I guess those lyrics that Ray Parker, Jr. sang were true: "When you think you're fooling her, she just might be fooling you. She can fool around just like you do."

When she came out of the bathroom, I asked her about the guy, and if she was having an affair. She said yes, and that all of the things that she wanted me to do, he was doing for her. Sounds familiar, doesn't it? I know what you are thinking, and you are correct. You reap what you sow…..karma….what goes around comes around…. do unto others as you would have them do unto you. Whatever the case was, it caught up with me, and I have to live with the fact that I have had two failed marriages, both of which I am fully responsible for allowing to fail.

She wanted out of the marriage, and I couldn't blame her, because I was still controlling, and she didn't love me anymore. I would've left me, also. After seven years, we separated in 2006, but our hearts were somewhere else long before that. I failed to see that she was an adult. She needed me, and I wasn't there for her, emotionally or physically. I forgot that she could make her own decisions, without me controlling her every move. I treated her like a child, and I paid the price.

Chapter 9
THE EARLY DAYS

When I was younger, I didn't have a voice in our house. My stepfather would tell me to shut up every time I wanted to explain myself, especially if he didn't agree with me. I realize, now, that I exhibited that same dominance over my wife. I kept her locked away in a state of emotional isolation, and it resulted in a lot of trauma to us both.

My stepfather was a drinker, smoker and liar, and I did not respect him. I didn't want to be like my stepfather, yet I became just like him. He was always yelling and didn't know how to manage his emotions. I wish I had been able to remove the mask long enough to seek help. Instead, I continued to create a web of destruction affecting not only myself, but also the people I loved.

I grew up trying to fit in with the other kids, never really taking ownership of my own identity. In an attempt to build status, I hung out with some of the toughest kids in school, but these were some of the same kids that used to pick on me. They're idea of fun was running through the hallways, picking fights and being a bully, but I had aspirations of being a professional basketball player or an actor. I was actively involved in theatre and even starred in a few school plays. I was headed in the right direction with my life, or so I thought, but part of me longed to just be "one of the guys." Being a leader was not on the agenda—I continued to be a follower. If my crew was late for class, so was I. If my crew wanted to jump on some kid for absolutely no reason, I would join them. My GPA dove to 1.5. I realize, now, that I was actually participating in gang activity. My grades were terrible and I was no longer motivated about my future.

In retrospect, I was having issues with my own insecurities. My smart-aleck-know-everything attitude continued well into my adulthood, and is still something I battle. This behavior is indicative of the fear and jealousy out of which I operate: fear of failing, fear of not being liked, fear of not fitting in with the guys, fear of not being smart enough. The only things I thought I was good at were playing sports and chasing girls. Girls gave me a sense of confidence, because they would respond to me in a way that was gentle, kind and pleasant. I knew that they liked me, and the more girls that I had, the better I felt about myself, which was what I needed to compensate for the lack of attention I received at home.

I remember getting evicted from houses on a regular basis and living out of hotels. For the life of me, I couldn't figure out how a man that went to work everyday was incapable of keeping a roof over our heads. To make matters worse, I didn't even know he was my stepfather until I was fifteen years old.

At age 17, I ran away from home. I hated my stepfather, and I started looking into going to college, but my grades weren't good enough. The next best thing was the military. I graduated high school in 1986. In July of that same year, I went into the United States Marines Corps. I was extremely happy about the move. I would finally be on my own. But it was at that time that my life would get turned upside down.

During the first week of boot camp, I realized that I couldn't handle people yelling at me. It wasn't so much the drill instructors, but the guy in my unit who was supposed to be the lead or the platoon guide. In my eyes, he was a snitch, always telling on me. The truth was that I wasn't doing what I was supposed to be doing. I wanted to play the tough role. I started to rebel so much that I disrupted the flow of boot camp. I would yell at the so-called "guide", then the drill instructors would get involved, and I yelled at them. Of course, they yelled back—what a spectacle I made of myself! But there was one drill instructor that I will never forget. Staff Sergeant Hunter pulled me aside and talked to me like a man. His words that day would never leave me. He told me that I needed to learn how to play the game, and that I had the ability to make it happen and be successful. I got what he was saying, for the time being anyway. The problem with that scenario was that I pretended to do the right thing, but never really let it sink into my mindset. What I remember most about our conversation was when he told me that I could make it, and to keep my head up. As a young kid who had been running from my problems with no direction, that advice meant everything to me. There I was, acting like a fool, trying to be tough, and I was completely blowing it. I had never had a man talk to me that way or encourage me like that, and it was those words that would get me through boot camp, which was no small feat. I saw guys cutting their wrists, trying just to get kicked out of boot camp. I was even more grateful for those words from a strong man. But not even Staff Sergeant Hunter could prepare me for what I was getting ready to embark upon.

After boot camp, I went on leave for ten days, to gear up for my first duty station in Okinawa, Japan. I was excited, looking forward to a new place, new life and new adventure. When I arrived, everything was new to me, with the exception of my attitude, lack of experience in life and the mask that I was wearing to hide my anger and my tears. I didn't know then how much those things mattered. Upon joining up with this new unit in Japan, I was introduced to the real world, and was brought face to face with racism. I was also dealing with the fact that I wasn't as mentally strong as I led on to be. I pretended to know how to handle each new experience. I tried, unsuccessfully, to brush off comments from my first sergeant, like, "If you people don't like the way I'm running this unit, write your congressman!" It was comments like that that started killing me softly. The only way I knew how to handle anything was by running away. Instead of dealing with the issues at hand, I went A.W.O.L.

I went to an air force base called Kadina, near Camp Foster, where I was based. There, I laid with a woman, contemplating whether or not to go to work that day. I didn't. I showed up at the end of the day, and was greeted by my staff sergeant. He asked me where I had been and I explained that I needed some time to think. My punishment for taking unauthorized leave was fourteen days on barracks restriction. During that time, I wasn't allowed to leave the unit, and I had to work desk duty for 14 days straight. That probably would've been a good time to ask for help, but I didn't. Instead, I continued to wear the "I'm in control" mask, all the way back to the States. I still had no idea how to deal with the racism I encountered regularly, so once again, I went A.W.O.L.—this time for 28 days. I floated around Compton, California, and finally landed at my sister's house, doing absolutely nothing with my life and writing six hundred dollars' worth of bad checks.

When I finally returned to the base, I was greeted by the military police, placed under arrest, put into handcuffs and hauled off to the Brig. All I did there was eat, shine boots and work out. On my 28th day of Brig time, I was released back into my unit. I told the guys that it was nothing to do time there, as if I should get some type of award for it. I continued to make ridiculous decisions along the way, like getting into an altercation with another marine. He called me a name, and I responded by getting in his space and striking him in the face. Afterwards, I paraded around singing a rap song by NWA: *"The boys in the hood are always hard/ come popping that s—t/we'll pull your card"*. Over and over, I sang these words, as if I were waiting to be acknowledged as one of these "hard" boys from the hood. A couple of days later, I was visited by the military police who placed me under arrest again, this time for assault.

Once again I was locked up, but this time I was court marshaled and kicked out of the military with a bad conduct discharge. By now, I felt like a complete failure. The last thing I heard from that first sergeant was that I wasn't going to accomplish anything with that type of discharge. Full of anger, I bought right into that mentality. Every time I applied for a job, I excluded that part of my past. I walked around with my head down, depressed. Nothing was going right for me, and I had to figure out what I was going to do with my life. Since those days, I've tried to get that discharge upgraded, to no avail. I have a bad conduct discharge on my record, and the responsibility lies solely on me. I will have to live with that for the rest of my life.

Despite all that I had been through, I couldn't give up on my life. I thought that I would turn the tide by chasing my lifelong dream of a career in rap music. Reciting and writing came easy for me. I would stay up all night sometimes, writing lyrics and rapping in front of the mirror. For whatever reason, I thought that if I made it, my pain would go away, and other people would praise me for doing something great. But because I never faced my real issues, my music was just a band-aid, when I actually needed surgery. No matter what I did, no matter where I ran, I couldn't get away from me. Still, I felt that if I stayed busy, I wouldn't have to deal with the rejection, loneliness, uncertainty and hurt that had taken up residence in my life.

In the early nineties, I was doing rap shows and searching for a record deal. I worked tirelessly to try to make my dream come true. Then, one day, my manager called me and told me that R&B singer, Ray Parker, Jr. was looking for a rapper to feature on one of the songs for his new album—he wanted to audition me for the rap part and I jumped at the chance. My producer and I went to the studio where we met producer, Ollie Brown and Ray. They played a series of songs that needed lyrics. When they played a song called "Love, Sex and Money", I knew it was the perfect song. I already had an idea of what I wanted to say, and my producer and I went to work on the lyrics. When we were finished, we were offered compensation to put out an album, however, they wanted 100% of the publishing rights, which, in my mind, is the equivalent of selling your soul to the devil. I had worked so hard for that opportunity, and I really wanted it, but I think that I was doing it for the wrong reasons. All along, I wanted to prove to my father that I could make it, and that I didn't need his help. I had already figured out who was getting a cut, and who was going to get cut out if I had made some big money.

I was dealing with an even bigger issue, however. God was tugging on me to change my life and my lyrics, and "Love, Sex and Money" didn't exactly qualify as a gospel tune. Trying to figure out what God was trying to do with me was frustrating. Was He calling me to preach? To teach? How could I work in ministry when I couldn't trust people? I wasn't even living right. I loved sleeping around with the different ladies, and I still enjoyed partying. Back then, all women could do for me was satisfy me. I didn't need or want any friends. I realize, now, that I didn't want anybody getting too close because it would be too painful to deal with if they just walked out of my life. I wondered why God would be trying to get my attention, but I finally succumbed to His voice, rejected the contract and ended up back in the church. The urge to sleep around, however, was still a big issue for me.

Chapter 10
CHURCH LUST

Church was full of beautiful women. White, Black, Asian, Latina—whatever the preference, it was there for the picking. I needed to change my life, but I wasn't sure how. All I knew was that I had to find a way. I set up an appointment to meet the pastor, who didn't tell me anything I didn't already know. Basically, he reminded me that I was a man, and as such, I would always be prone to the temptation of sex—those urges were a part of being a man. In order to keep my urges under control, I would need to have a prayer life. I did what he suggested and increased my prayer activity, but no matter how hard I tried to fight it, I soon found myself giving in to the same urges once again. Through it all, I felt that God was calling me to the ministry. My calling was reconfirmed through another minister who told me I had testimony that could change lives. I wanted to take walking a righteous path seriously, however, I couldn't stop operating as a whore long enough to make any real impact. For a while, I successfully played both roles. On Sunday morning, I was the model minister, but I was still easily influenced—still getting involved with the ladies in the congregation. I took being a player to a new level. Looking the part on the outside did nothing to change who I was inside, and I was still looking for a change.

Running from life, as usual, I decided to move to Denver, Colorado with my best friend. I needed a change, but I still had not embraced the idea that change comes from within, and not from a change in your zip code. Chasing women was still my drug of choice, and my addiction followed me to Denver and almost led to my early demise.

Chapter 11
SAVING FACE

In Denver, I met another young lady with whom I began to have sex on a regular basis. One day, she started telling me about her child's father. She told me that he was the jealous type, which held little significance for me—I knew I could handle him, and if he started anything, he'd be in for a beat-down. Just then, the telephone rang, and it was him. He heard me talking in the background, and asked her who I was. After a moment of silence, she told him I was a friend; he clearly did not want me there. I could tell from her end of the conversation that he was interrogating her, so I fired back, telling him that he didn't control her house, and that he should worry about his own business. That was the last of it…until the day he dropped by to pick up his child.

When I pulled up in front of the house, he was outside, sitting in his car. I saw him, he saw me, and we stared each other down. Although we had never seen each other before, I already knew what kind of car he drove. I asked him what the hell he was looking at, and he said something like, "I'm looking at you, Punk," so I approached his car. He got out and a fight ensued. I threw the first punch and knocked him out. In the projects, there are always a lot of people standing around outside, so I played to the crowd, keeping in mind that I was new to the area. I had to let it be known that I was the wrong cat to be messing with. In the hood, credibility is everything.

Later that day, the Denver Police were knocking at her door. Apparently, he had called the police on me, which was the last thing I expected to happen. In the hood, when you fight and lose, you suck it up like a man and go home, but you do *not* call the police. I was read my rights, cuffed and taken to jail. On the way there, I explained to the police that he started the whole fiasco, and suggested that they check his criminal background. They did and found that he had a huge record. I, on the other hand, had never been arrested. By the time we got to the jail, they were already planning to release me. I was there for five minutes and left with no charges filed. My best friend picked me up and he took me back to the young lady's house. By the time we had arrived at the projects, I still felt that I had to show people that I was the man, so the bragging began. I told my story to everyone who would listen.

On the drive back, my friend had mentioned a house party that was taking place that evening in Greeley, Colorado. We agreed to meet up later and go. While at the party, I met another girl who had recently broken up with her boyfriend. He was the jealous type also, according to her, but I began to communicate with her on the telephone, anyway. You would think

I'd have learned my lesson, but I hadn't. We agreed to go out on a date, and we had a very good time. At the end of the date, she invited me back to her place, where we talked for a while, and then, ultimately, slept together.

I remembered that I had left my gun in the car, so I ran outside to get it, in case someone tried to break into my car. I returned, and put the gun under the pillow. Within 15 minutes, her ex was knocking on the door.

She opened the door in her robe and I remember thinking, "What are you doing, you dumb female?" I could hear him demanding to know if she had another man there. My finger was resting on the trigger of my gun, which was still under the pillow. I waited for him to approach me—I was ready to kill that day, if I had to. Suddenly, he barged through the bedroom door, and all I could think about was how difficult it is to reason with someone who is in a rage like that. Without provocation, he turned on his heels, directed his verbal assault toward her and then left. If I had been a true, ruthless killer, I wouldn't have given it a second thought. But as I calmed down, all I could think about was how quickly my life could have changed—the consequences I'd have had to face if things had gone wrong.

I guess the saying is true: If you don't stand for something, you will fall for anything. If it weren't for the grace of God, who knows where I would be? I guess one of the most important lessons life has taught me is that you must always get to know yourself. Take a little time to assess where you are, and be willing to make the necessary adjustments so that you can have a productive life.

Chapter 12
COMPUTER "LOVE"?

I am now single, and still battling this spirit of manipulation and loneliness—still a pretender. The only difference in my life these days is that I avoid having emotional attachments with women, so the only one who is still hurting is me. I have left the church and the ministry. I am hanging out with the enemy on a regular basis, with no accountability. I call it "free-lancing". I am still using women and pretending to be someone that I am not.

Just recently, I was on a dating website, browsing through the profiles of all the women, picking out who I would try to get a date with and, ultimately, manipulate into the bedroom. I found one—sent her an instant message, and she responded. I started the conversation off with a simple "Hello". She told me that I was handsome. I knew then that I was going to get her into bed. I checked my mask in the mirror and went to work. I told her how pretty she was, and I said things to keep her laughing and smiling. I call this the "build-up", because my next move was to get her on the telephone so she could hear my voice. Once I felt that she was comfortable, we exchanged numbers.

I knew what was going to happen, but it excited me nonetheless.

We talked, and I continued to woo her, telling her that I wanted her to see me on my web camera. I let her view me and began to slowly suck her into my game. I started using my charisma and my anointing from God to manipulate her. I recited poetry to her, and she liked it—she told me it turned her on. I started talking sexually to her, and before I knew it, I was doing sexual things on my cam for her. She started telling me how much she wanted me, which led me to tell her what I wanted her to do for me. She was touching herself on my command, and after we were done playing, I told her that I wanted to see her. She drove 50 miles to see me, and I wasn't about to disappoint her. We had great sex and I knew that once we were done, I wouldn't be interested in chatting with her anymore. I had won the challenge, enjoyed the prize and now it was time for a new adventure.

From that point on, the pretender was on the prowl. I had become addicted to the Internet. It enabled me to transform myself into anyone I wanted to be. One night I was perusing the dating site and spotted the profile of a beautiful young lady who emphasized that she wanted a thug. I immediately changed my profile to match what she was looking for, pretending to be someone that I was not. It wasn't unusual for me to flip the script and pretend to be a different person, so I was quite comfortable with that role. The interesting thing about this is that I didn't even blink. I put on the mask of the pretender so quickly that it would make your head spin. I played the role so well that I could have gotten paid for it. This has been the story of my life, and now I have to figure out how to find *me* so I can be that person that I was destined to be.

Chapter 13
THE STORY OF THE FIANCÉS

I've had so many fiancés that I've lost count. A proposal, to me, meant that I could have sex whenever I wanted. All I had to do was to convince the woman that she was "The One". It worked—numerous times. I'd have sex with them over and over and over again, and afterwards, I would go to church, fall on my knees and repent. I would cry my eyes out, and then I would get up and do the same thing all over again.

I was sincere with God. I didn't want to behave the way that I was, but I couldn't stop. When I grew bored with a woman's lovemaking, I'd dump her and move on to the next conquest—different name, same game. Most of the women that I proposed to were members of my church. Sunday after Sunday, they watched me pray for people with the power of the Holy Ghost, when in truth, I had no power at all. I was too busy pretending that I was the man—too busy faking. These women watched me "ministering" to people, while all along, the whole church knew that I was a male whore.

Finally, I sat myself down. No more praying for folks, no more pretending to minister. I was a fraud—not that I wasn't a minister, not even that I wasn't called. I was a minister that had a problem—a problem which I still didn't feel I could confide in anyone. I started to feel the guilt of manipulating the people, and it was taking its toll on my mind, heart and spirit. I was slowly losing my soul to the devil. It didn't matter that I had good intentions to stop, because the women at the church were not helping. They wanted to get married so bad that they would do almost do anything to get my last name. The more dirt that they heard about me the more they wanted to sleep with me. I felt like a celebrity. There I was, sitting *myself* down, and women were still throwing their panties at me, which goes to show you that pretenders can be male or female. Nevertheless, I took the bait like a fish that hasn't eaten in a week. I was a disgrace, a failure and I was being taking advantage of by my own weakness. "When will it end?" is what I kept asking myself. I am still asking that question as I write this book

Chapter 14
THE TRUST FACTOR

I trust no one. I'm not sure who is on my team and who is against me. Letting down my guard is not an option. People around me are always trying to figure out why I am so cold. To be honest, *I'm* not even sure. I keep people at a distance; I don't give them a chance to get to know me. Maybe I am afraid that they won't like me, or maybe I can't reconcile that part of me that can be verbally abusive towards others. It's hard for me to admit because my step father was an abuser, but I make no excuses.

My mother is so precious and beautiful. I would never want anyone to hurt her. Unfortunately, I treat the women who love me differently—I hurt them and call them names, and cut them off without letting them have a voice.

I think about a woman I once dated who I yelled at and called names—I treated her so badly, and now she's in a relationship with a woman. She said that women are more nurturing, understanding and better listeners. She now runs a whorehouse. The fact that my treatment of her is a contributing factor in why she started exploring women is hard to embrace, but I accept the blame. Of course, it's also possible that she has always been attracted to women, and was just pretending to be attracted to me.

Sometimes I look at myself and the way that I am and get disgusted. I have relied on my looks for years, but never relied on being truthful to myself. A lot of people put on facades in order to hide the pain and cover up their flaws or sins. I lay awake at night wondering if I will ever be all that I believe that I can be, or if this is how my life will always be. Is God above going to help me get through this? I'm tired of hurting women. I want to be a positive life force, a motivator who encourages others. I want to be the good listener.

Chapter 15
THE NEED FOR CONTROL

The need for control plagues me, and the people around me are the recipients of it. I am a supervisor at my job and my supervisory style is "my way or the highway". I can get out of line with this power trip, to the point that I get angry at myself. People have asked me questions and I would cut them off before they could even get the question completely out of their mouths. Then, to make matters worse, I would attempt to answer the question that I thought that they were going to ask, and more often than not, my response would be wrong. I wouldn't allow this behavior to manifest around people who didn't know me. Instead, I hid it and played the good guy, pretending that I had it all together.

I dominate like a dictator, and because I don't understand why I do it, I can't control it. My secretary would try to tell me things that were important for me to know, and I would tell her that I didn't want to hear it—my arrogance breeds ignorance. This is the same type of behavior I exhibited around my friends, literally cursing my friends out when we would have a heated debate. I would get downright mad because I always had to be right. Sometimes I would be wrong and know that I was wrong and continue the argument anyhow. But the hothead in me didn't allow me to cease fire. I've even treated my former girlfriends the same way. I've loud-talked them, and said things to make them cry, intentionally sometimes, just to let them know that I was in control. One ex-girlfriend was visiting me at my mother's house and, try as I might, she wouldn't allow me to control her. When I raised my voice, she'd raise hers, and her attempts to stand up for herself annoyed me, so I hit her in the face and left her with two swollen eyes. She responded by chasing me down the street with a butcher knife, all because of my control issues and anger—all because I wanted to be right.

I have turned so many people against me that, at one time, half of my own staff wouldn't even talk to me, while others only spoke because they had to. This was self-created, and I have no one else to blame but myself. One of my colleagues called me the Black Hitler, and although it seemed funny at the time, it was painful and shocking that this was how I was perceived! To be compared to a man who killed so many was symbolic of how I was emotionally killing everyone around me. I am disgusted with myself for possessing the talents of a leader, but being too emotionally damaged to exercise my skills. I am stuck with myself and my dysfunctional ways, and somehow, I have to get free of myself and seek out the healing that has eluded me for most of my life. I need and want help. I need to talk to someone who can free me of my need to be something that I am not, while teaching me to embrace who I am. I have to relinquish all control—give it up, surrender my fears and rebuild the foundation of my manhood. It's an arduous task, but one I must complete before I die and leave this earth. My legacy cannot be that of a controller and a pretender.

Chapter 16
THE NEED FOR ATTENTION

I am addicted to attention. In fact, I demand it. I am needy, when it comes right down to it. I have met women on the street and brought them home to have sex with them and when we were done having sex, I would tell them that I needed for them to hold me. I would roll over away from them, and I would literally put their arm around me while I slept. My grandmother says that this need stems from not being held and attended to when I was a baby. At my most vulnerable, I am a little boy trapped in a grown man's body. My ex-wife once told me that I was too much work, and that she wasn't the one to help me heal from the pain that I had experienced. She said it was too much for her—the anger, late-night crying and depression. I had to identify my fear of being alone. Or my even greater fear: being an outstanding individual and citizen, full of hope sunshine and goodness.

Chapter 17
CHURCH PIMPIN'

Beware of another clergy clique—church pimps. These are among the biggest pretenders of them all. Don't be fooled—these guys and gals come in all shapes, sizes and colors, and their mission is to bring you into their fold. They don't mean anyone any good. I have seen pimps in the church taking notes on which girl they were going to turn out and add to their list of hookers or call girls. I was associated with a young lady, a stripper in a club, who came to church faithfully every Sunday. I am not putting her down—just acknowledging her existence. A lot of women in church have low self-esteem issues. They've been abused, misused and deceived; the type of woman who is easy to feed on. Pimps will pursue someone with a victim's mentality over a strong mind any day. We don't have time for all of the madness that comes with a confident woman.

These pimps are praying for you, passing the plate around in the church and preaching the gospel, while calling themselves deacons, ushers, pastors and ministers. The church is like a club—seek and you shall find it. Pimps, hoes, embezzlers, liars, backstabbers, adulterers—you name it, churches have got it. Go to a club the night before on a Saturday and then show up to church on Sunday, and tell me who you see. The same folks that were drinking, smoking, cursing and grinding the night before are the same folks that are laying hands on you and calling the devil a liar. Know who the pretenders are; use your spiritual discernment, if you have any. This is not a referendum on the church. There are tons of folks in the church who are faithful and sincere. But there are also pretenders in church and they need to be dealt with, revealed. Men and women alike are being taking advantage of in the church, and the culprits are the pretenders dressed in sheep's clothing. I know pastors who have embezzled your hard-earned money, preaching the gospel and reciting every scripture in the Bible that encourages you to give. I was one of those guys teaching on giving. But I was doing more taking than giving, and not just money—hearts, souls and emotions—luring them right out of their innocence. That's what pretenders do. I have been at the table with pastors talking about hoes in the church—who is fine and who they are going to sleep with—the Pimp Pretender Movement. It wasn't about the people, it was about us. Our selfishness with no regard, compassion or feelings for the people we hurt in the process. They tell you that you can't borrow money from the church, because they're not a bank. Yet they'll accept your deposits without blinking an eye. Watch out for guys like me, fast-talking, good-looking guys who promise you the world.

Pay attention, or you might miss him. He just might be the one in the preacher's robe, the deacon or the usher. Watch out and ask questions.

Chapter 18
ANGER AND BITTERNESS

The anger and resentment that I have for my former pastors still exists. Some people ask me how I let these feelings stay with me for so long, and the simple answer is that I never took the steps necessary to heal. I was hurt emotionally by my stepfather, so I became very skeptical when it came to letting people into my circle. However, there were some men who I allowed in, and they became like fathers to me, and I am not sure I should have put them into that role, but I did. I opened up to them, told them all of the things that I was battling, and every little intricate thing about me, only to be let down.

My first pastor was a very nice guy, a non-confrontational type, someone I found easy to relate to. I would run to him all the time with my issues. When I would sleep around, I would run to the altar to ask for forgiveness, and to the pastor to seek guidance. Sometimes, he would invite me to his house to counsel me. I cried and completely let myself go. I wanted to do the right thing. At one point, I would have been willing to take a bullet for him. This was the type of bond that I had with this man. I was comfortable with him and he vowed that he would never tell anyone else of my issues. There wasn't anything that I felt I couldn't tell him. I gave tithes and offerings to the church faithfully; I wanted to do everything I could to support this ministry because I believed in it and the pastor, and bought into the idea that this church was about change. I felt like this was the type of ministry I could really get involved with. I had finally found someone who cared about me, someone who wasn't going to hurt me. After all of the support that I had given to the church and the time spent running errands for him, the time had come for me to step out into what I believed to be a move of God.

My wife and I set up an appointment with the pastor and his wife. We wanted to let them know about the vision that I had. I was starting my own Christian clothing line. I was excited and my wife was supportive. We were fired up, only to be cooled off by the pastor's demeanor and his attitude. It was as though he had more important things to do, than to hear me rattle on about my "so-called vision". In fact, I remember him making the statement that I only had a few minutes to speak because he had a construction meeting to attend. He was building a new church, and God forbid that his vision didn't come to pass. I was deeply hurt that the man that I had confided in and trusted so much could only spare a few minutes to hear me out.

He acted like my vision was so small, compared to his, and to be made to feel that I wasn't worthy to even get a full meeting with my mentor was very painful.

I was devastated, and my wife knew it. I recall my wife saying that it seemed as if he didn't give a damn. I agreed that she was exactly right, and that was the last time I had communications with that pastor. That was the day that I stopped paying tithes, because I refused to support a ministry whose pastor only cared about his own interests. I know that most people would say that you are supposed to pay tithes to God, but in reality, I was paying to build up a ministry that I just didn't believe in anymore, so we left.

I promised myself that I would never open up to anyone again, especially not to a pastor. I felt that all of them were about making money, and when the money stopped coming in, so did their support and guidance. The good thing, though, is that I did not give up on God. I was angry and bitter to the point that just the mention of church pissed me off. When people would invite me to church, I would literally go off. I would demand that they provide me with a reason that would convince me that I should go. I would contend that the church is in your heart, not the four walls of a building. My perspective when it came to churches was that they take advantage of the less fortunate. Pastors, in my opinion, tried to hustle money from people on a fixed income. I was irate and ready to hit the roof at any moment. I knew pastors that were embezzling money and leaving the church bone dry. I really just wasn't ready to go to any more church buildings, and began asking people to refrain from inviting me.

I even tried watching the ministries on television. Big mistake! There were preachers selling "anointed" handkerchiefs, blessed water, and any other "holy charm" that the viewers would spend their hard-earned money on—and they did! I thought that I was pretending to be someone I wasn't, but these guys seemed to have it down to a science. Then, I saw a couple of programs featuring a certain individual (I won't mention any names) who was blowing on people, which seemed to cause them to fall to the floor. I didn't know who to believe in—if anyone. I felt that I could get the same brand of "honesty" from politicians. In fact, as I watch political-themed programming, I have begun to recognize them as pretenders, too. They are people selling a dream, and once they're in office, you find out how empty their promises were. Damn! I can't win.

I know some of you are saying that I am just angry, and you are right. I'm angry at Jim Jones, Jimmy Swaggart, Jim Bakker, and all of the rest of these clowns who have lied to people and then jumped into their Bentley Coupes, while Sis. So-and-so is sitting on the front row, hungry. Whatever happened to helping the needy and being there for the poor? Now they are left to help themselves.

I once had a pastor friend that used to talk about me behind my back; what a leader! To top it off, he would brag about how much money he made from the church. In fact, I stopped associating with that type of person, from ministers to deacons, and anybody else who was not sincere about God. It was sickening and I couldn't take it anymore, so I left the building. That's why I say the church is in your heart and that these guys are pretenders. I have never yet heard a preacher say that God told them that he or she should give the congregation a thousand dollars. It's always the other way around. "Give," they say, "and God is going to bless you." They make it seem that God is money-hungry. Why is your blessing always predicated on how much money you give? I don't buy it. Even I used to preach that nonsense at one time. Now that I see it for all of the pretending and manipulation that is involved, I think I must have looked like a crazed maniac with all of the dirt and schemes I have come up with. I don't want anyone to get confused, and I am not suggesting that anyone leaves the building, or that you start doubting your pastor—he or she might be the exception. I am definitely not suggesting that you give up on God, because He is not the issue. We, the pretenders, are the issue. What I am suggesting is that you be honest, and ask yourself why you are attending your assembly. What has God put on your heart to do, and are you being honest with yourself? It's time to use wisdom, to care for God's people and to engage in effective dialogue when we disagree with one another. The time has also come for us to take off our masks and stop pretending that everything is okay with us, and seek the counseling of others that have our best interest at heart. If we are true to ourselves, then we will find freedom and so many others around us will be set free. I have to admit, though, that I am not all the way there yet. I am one of those ministers who has destroyed, or at least damaged, a lot of people, and I have to be accountable for that. To all of my other friends in the gospel, let's keep it real with the people we deal with. Let's stop robbing and stealing and manipulating the truth and God's word for our own gain. There is no doubt that we are responsible, and accountable for His people. The question is, will you change your ways and accept the truth?

Chapter 19
PLAYING THE FOOL

I don't have any kids, but at one time, I thought I did. The child's mother told me that I was the father, and I took her word for it, and began to help raise this child. You are probably wondering why I didn't at least get a DNA test, and I wonder that myself now. Let me go back to the beginning. I met a young lady at the bowling alley one night and we exchanged numbers. We started talking on the telephone late at night. I was digging her conversation, and she was digging mine. Although I really wasn't attracted to her, I knew that I could sleep with her. I knew that that was wrong, and I was using her from the beginning, because she had something I wanted—sex. I figured as long as I wasn't seen with her by the wrong people, I could maintain my reputation of dating only the prettiest women. So I came up with a plan to hang out with her only at nighttime, and only in places where no one knew me. If we went to a movie, it was away from my neighborhood. Once we arrived, I would let her walk into the theater, and I would stop at the bathroom to prevent anyone from thinking that we were together. I knew that by the time I got back, it would be dark and no one would see us anyway. After the movie, we would stop at the store for drinks and go back to my place to have sex over and over until we were just tired of doing it.

This continued for a few months, until one day, she told me she was pregnant. I wasn't upset—in fact, I was happy. I wasn't particularly happy that she was the mother, but I was a man getting ready to have my first-born. I wasn't even thinking about a DNA test or anything like that, because I had been with this girl almost every day since we met, so there was no question in my mind. But, the more time we spent together, we discovered that we didn't get along all that well. We began to argue in a big way. Despite our differences, however, something bigger was at stake here. She was receiving a large amount of money from a grandparent, and all I knew was that I wanted some of that money, and I was willing to play the nice guy until she received it. At that point, I would do whatever it took. I was seen with her everywhere, my pride not nearly as important as it used to be. She was about two months pregnant when the money came in—about $20,000, I think. I took her to the bank personally. We went to the Honda dealer, where she bought a Volkswagen Jetta, and I got a Honda Accord. I made sure that it was registered in my name so that if she got mad at me, she couldn't take the car away. After I got what I wanted, I started distancing myself from her. I told her that I didn't want the baby, and encouraged her to have an abortion and leave me alone. We didn't see each other again for about seven months, when she called me and told me that she had just had the baby. I went to the hospital to visit her and "our" new healthy baby boy. I must admit that I was excited, and I stayed in the kid's life for about a year. The stress and the aggravation with her new boyfriend and her attitude became too much, and I felt like I was going to get myself in trouble if I stayed in that situation. It had come to the point where she and I would get into it and I would spit on her like she was a piece of trash, and I wanted to blast her man off of the face of this planet. I was becoming over protective and angry. I decided that instead of letting my anger get the best of me and cause me to end up in a worse situation, I would just leave.

I didn't hear from the child or the mother again until I walked into a nail shop one day to visit a friend, and there they were. We talked for a few minutes, and even exchanged phone numbers. She told me that she didn't want anything from me, but that I could come by and visit the child anytime I wanted. I loved picking him up and taking him over to visit my friends. I loved bragging about him. Then, one day I took him over to my mother's house. When out of nowhere my mother said, "He doesn't look like you." I shrugged that off because just earlier that day, some people that I didn't know told me that he looked just like me. Besides, I was just really excited to have a son. His mother and I agreed that I would pick my son up from daycare on the days that he was supposed to spend the night with me. I arrived to pick him up one day, and the aid told me that his father had already picked him up. I told her that I was the baby's father, and was convinced that there must have been some mistake. Her boyfriend had picked up my son, and when I called the house, she was quite nonchalant. I asked where my son was and she told me that he was playing. I yelled at her about how worried I had been, and that she should have at least called me to tell me that he was being picked up. Then, in the background, I could hear her boyfriend playing with him, and I heard my son call him "Daddy". I was sick. I told her to get him ready because I was on my way, and she agreed. When I arrived, she started playing games, telling me that she wasn't sure that she wanted me to take him. I lost it, and told her that she better get him ready, or I was going to start tearing up the house. She ran inside, and I tried to go in after her. She yelled out to me that she had called the police, so I left as fast as possible. After that, I tried calling her, but to no avail. About a week later, I was served with a restraining order and child support papers. So I called her and told her that I wasn't going to pay one red cent, not realizing that they would garnish my wages. What happened to her telling me that she didn't want anything from me? Now, I can't even see the kid? This went on for about five years, and I never wanted to see her again. It was then that she made her mistake. She called me and told me that she was moving out of state with the baby, and the state where I lived required the permission of the non-custodial parent in order to take a child out of state.

I made it abundantly clear that I was not going to authorize that move, and furthermore, I told her that if she did go across state lines, that I would take her to court. By this time, the restraining order had long since expired. Of course she took my son across the state lines. I can be honest with you—I didn't want her to have to come back with the child, but as long as she was not going to let me see him, I wanted to stop paying child support. Well, she got the order to bring the child back, and that's when the phone started ringing. She agreed to drop the child support if I would allow her to take him out of state. I agreed on the condition that he would stay with me for a school year. We put our agreement into writing. By this time, we were both married, and my spouse was happy that we weren't paying anymore child support. She had seen the drama that I had gone through and was relieved that the whole ordeal was nearly over.

We picked him up at the airport, and I took him to see my mother, who maintained that he didn't look like me. This had never totally left my mind, so I requested a test through the court system, and was denied because they thought that I was trying to get out of my responsibility. At the suggestion of a friend, I ordered a DNA swab test on-line. I told him that we had to swab the inside of his mouth for the dentist for school. (Was I really supposed to tell him that I wasn't sure he was my son?) We mailed it off, and got the results back in a couple of weeks, during which time, I was on pins and needles. When I finally called and gave them the secret password, the lady said they had the results, and asked if I wanted them by phone or by mail. I wanted to know right then, although my heart was beating fast and my mouth was dry from the anticipation. The phone was silent for a moment, then she told me that it was 99.99% certain that the child was not mine.

My chin dropped from the shock, but I wasn't mad. Again, I was happy, and I couldn't wait to call his mother, right after I called mine. I asked his mother who his father was, and why she had let him call not one, but two men "Daddy", when she knew that neither of us was. I told her that she would tell him that I was not his father. At this point, I didn't care if I ever saw him again. I cared more about being away from her and not having to pay child support then I actually cared about the child. There was no connection for me with this child, and I'm not even sure that I loved him when I did think that he was mine. Maybe the uncertainty of not knowing if I was his father was an issue, or maybe it was the fact that there was so much drama that I just wanted the whole nightmare to go away. To be honest, though, I don't think I was a very good father. I used to yell at him all the time and whip him. I never really spent any quality time with him, never really took his feelings into consideration, never set any expectations for him. It is just now occurring to me, and it is devastating to have to accept.

Sometimes, I look in the mirror and ask myself why I am so cold, and the truth is, I don't know. I can only imagine what his memories of me are. I'm almost certain that the kid hates me, and there is no telling what his mother has told him about me. I haven't talked to him in years, and still have no real desire to do so. It's not that I wouldn't like to see him, but I think I am afraid of the outcome, or the repercussions. Or what he might think of me. How ironic, though, that I became exactly what I said I never would—an abuser. What started out as a little sex and a game, turned into a real-life fiasco, and all of my pretending has caused hurt and pain and dissension, once again.

Chapter 20
MY BELIEF SYSTEM

I am often asked about my belief system, and with the way I have conducted myself in the past and the present, I can't really blame people for wondering. I usually tell them that I believe what most people believe: that we should treat people the way we want to be treated; that life is about giving, sacrificing and compromising; that there is a God, and that He is supreme. I also let them know that I am a Christian, saved, sanctified and filled with the Holy Ghost. That's when it usually gets sticky, and they begin to look at me incredulously. I can almost hear them thinking, "Oh, another 'Christian'. Everyone is a Christian, but they all do their own thing." Unfortunately, in many cases, they are right. They have encountered the "Christians" who hang out at the clubs, commit adultery, drink alcohol, lie, deceive and manipulate

I've done all of these things, and am still doing some of them to this day. Even to myself, I have to admit, that sounds like a sinner who is pretending to be a Christian. How can I help someone else come to Christ and better their lives if I'm caught in the same traps that they are in? Who is going to listen to and trust a minister like me? To be honest, I wouldn't listen to a fool like me, either. My mother didn't raise me to behave like this. In fact, she preached against it. I remember her telling me a long time ago to leave all of those fast girls alone. She wanted me to understand that they were "hot to trot" and that I needed to slow down, before I got one of them pregnant, or something worse happened.

As you know, I didn't listen to that advice. But Mom was right. I didn't get anyone pregnant, but I have dealt with a whole lot of drama, all because I didn't take heed to Mom's advice. We didn't see eye to eye all the time, but I can say that Nora Holliday is a giver. She always tries to help wherever she can, whether it's picking folks up for church, cooking for her school, or volunteering at her church. And if you asked her to sing, she would jump right on that! But her charity began at home. I can recall my mother scraping together her last few pennies to feed us. When we played on the basketball team, we couldn't get the Nikes that we wanted, but she made sure we had some tennis shoes on our feet. My brother and I didn't understand it at first. We complained that we wanted to wear the same clothes and shoes that the rest of the kids were wearing, not clothes from K-mart. But Mom gave all she had for my brother and me and even now, my mother is the same way. My brother and I have moved back in with Mom when we were struggling. Her door is always open to us, and she never changes. She taught us that if we are true to God, He will be true to us, so even though I am sure that some of the things in this book will be a little disappointing to her, I know that she will continue to tell me to dust off my feet and keep right on going. Even when we didn't want to hear it, my brother and I could count on her to tell us that we can't do anything without God, and in the back of our minds, we knew that she was telling the truth. So, yes, I grew up with and was taught those core values, I just haven't been living by them. My mother is not to blame. In fact, Mom, if you are reading this, I want you to know that you are a great mom. In fact, you are the mom of a lifetime, and no award would be just due for you. Make no mistake about it, these are the beliefs that make up my personal belief system, and they were instilled in me by my mother, who loves me unconditionally, just like the God she's always told me about. For those who are judging me right now, you would do better to pray for me. That is also part of my belief system.

Chapter 21
LIKE FATHER, LIKE SON

I often talk to my biological father about the women in his life, because I think I might find some insight into the reasons behind my out-of-control behavior. Sure enough, he has explained to me that he was the same way at one time, dating and sleeping with multiple women on a regular basis. Maybe that explains why he has five kids (that we know of), by four different mothers. In fact, my brother is one year younger than I am, and one of my sisters is just one month younger than I am.

My mother and stepmother would tell me how good-looking my dad is, and that he had a way with the women; that they were extremely attracted to his smile. I have seen it firsthand—women trying to latch on to my father and flirt with him. I must say, my father is still a good-looking man, and I think he uses that to his advantage. He knows when women are attracted to him and he plays on that—not to the point of using them, although he could if he wanted to. I mean, these women would cook for him, clean for him, they would even wash his dirty drawers if he asked them. But witnessing his charm, wit, quick responses and the ability to choose just the right words, I saw where I got it from.

My issue, though, is that I play on that attraction and take it to the next level, sort of like my father did back in his day. I allowed them to do the cooking, cleaning and dirty drawers-washing, and then bring me butter pecan ice cream. And for what? Just so these women could have the privilege of sleeping with me. I know I sound arrogant, and I almost can't stand it. But as much as I hated that about myself, most of the women I knew loved it. So, what was I supposed to do?

Just the other day, a woman told me that she was trying to figure out if I was sexy on accident or sexy on purpose. She added that I was cocky and arrogant, as if I haven't heard that before. Regardless, it strokes your ego and it makes you feel good to get compliments, but what I had become was disgusting and it leaves a bad taste in my mouth to think of it, even now. It seemed as if I couldn't get around this thing. Of course, I was still pretending that I liked these women, when I knew that I was not going to see them ever again once they left my house. I asked my father how he stopped chasing women. He said that he started going to church, got saved and began to work in the ministry. Well, if you have been paying any attention, then you know that that's where I got into trouble. Maybe the church is not the place for me, when it comes to my addiction. "In due time," my father said. "In due time. Stay busy and focus, and you will be fine." I guess considering the way Pops turned out, I don't mind this segment being called "Like Father, Like Son," because when it comes to getting victory over my indulgence in these affairs and escapades, I aspire to be just like him.

Chapter 22
IDENTIFYING A PRETENDER

Through my networking with others, people always seem to ask me, "How do you identify a pretender? What are some of the signs?" Sometimes it is very difficult to recognize a pretender, especially if the person has perfected their craft. In my case, I had done this for so long that I had it down to a tee. Lying with a straight face, manipulating and deceiving others with conviction—I was so good at it that I almost convinced myself that the things that were coming out of my mouth were true. But no one is perfect, and we all slip up from time to time. So there will always be a give-away or a sign, if you pay attention.

Let me give you a basic example: If you meet a guy who opens the door for you consistently when you meet, and then one day he stops opening doors, then you want to ask yourself if he is really who you thought he was. I must tell you, if opening the door for my companion is in me, then the doors will continue to be opened. If it's not, then those signs will show as well. I know some of you are thinking that this is a small thing, but it's the little things that lead us to know the big things. I know I used to open the door for my companion, then I stopped, not because I got tired, but because I was pretending to be a gentlemen who liked opening doors. She let that slide, and soon, I lost interest in going to the movies we used to go to on Saturdays when we first met. That's because I didn't like doing that in the first place. So your man has lost interest in doing the things that you used to enjoy doing together, and you say it's a small thing, so you look over that. Have you noticed your spouse's work days are getting longer? He used to get home at 5:00 pm, now he is arriving at 8:00 pm, and he has long since stopped calling ahead or offering explanations when he gets home. There's a good chance that he's not working. Go ahead and give him a call to ask him how his day is going at work.

Once you give a pretender an inch, he or she will take a yard; it is up to you not to tolerate it. You have to remember that most of the time if you have a feeling that something is going on, it is. And a true telltale sign is if, when you ask him about the long hours, he gets irate with you, as if you did something wrong. Don't let that person manipulate you and turn the situation around on you. That's what I did. I would come home sometimes at 4:00am, and my wife would ask me about it, and I would try to justify it by saying, "You go out with your girlfriends and come home late at night or in the morning!" The difference there was that she told me before she did it. I didn't do that because I was out driving around in the streets looking for women, so stick to your guns.

I am not telling you to start spying on your spouse or friend, but you do have to be aware of what's going on around you. Don't be deceived and manipulated by people or by your companion. I pretended to be all of the things my spouse wanted in a man just long enough to get in, and when I got what I wanted, I went back to being who I was. Women must set boundaries for themselves. You should never let a guy like me just get away with treating you badly or saying inappropriate things to you. Remember, if you let me get away with it once, I am most likely going to try it again.

Another thing that I noticed about the women that I have encountered was that they were too ambitious where I was concerned. I mean, if you tell me you like me or you want to go out with me, seeming to almost beg for my attention, then it's going to be real easy for me to run game on you. I played on the emotions of the women that I dealt with, so when they came into the situation already emotionally invested, it made it really easy for me to do whatever I wanted. It's almost like giving someone the key to your apartment and telling them to make themselves at home without laying down any ground rules. When you meet someone, set the boundaries and pay attention. And remember to watch out for the signs of a pretender.

Chapter 23
CAN YOU HANDLE THE TRUTH?

Most people *think* they want to hear the truth. But when it comes down to it, they truly can't handle it. For example, if a woman's asks me to be honest with her in our relationship, quoting the phrase "honesty is the best policy", I would agree. But what happens if I come to my wife or girlfriend and tell her that I don't love her anymore, but rather, I want to marry her brother because I am gay? How do you think she would handle it? Could you handle that? Imagine that I am in the church, acting a fool and cursing out the deacons and sleeping with the minister's wives and the deacon's girlfriends. How about me acting out and masturbating in the back row of the choir stand? Are you still with me? What if I am sleeping with my daughter? Would you still be able to forgive me?

Most of us take the low road—first, we put the person down and say how terrible they are, and then try to convince God that his or her sin is different from ours. Instead of us praying for such individuals, we gossip and spread rumors. If this is you, then you are part of the problem, which also means you have your own issues that you must deal with. I also haven't figured out how gossiping helps people solve their issues. Yes. I am talking to you, Mr. Christian Man and Ms. Christian Woman. How does it feel to know that you have been working for the devil? That you have not been assisting in helping with changing lives for the better? I know for a fact that I have been scrutinized and talked about, even thrown under the bus by people with the same issues. But they are spineless cowards because they don't have enough courage to step up and make a difference in this world. No one wants to be transparent—they would rather hide behind the mask and evade the truth. Am I describing you? If so, you are a pretender. Now, what is your next move?

We often say the world would be a better place if we would all take a look at ourselves and examine our ways. The problem is that most of us don't understand that in order for that to happen, we will have to go through a transformation, and things may become harder before they get any easier. They might get uglier before they get pretty. If you can handle all of this then maybe now you can change the man in the mirror.

Some would ask why I would write a book that is so transparent, one that blasted my conduct and put down my way of thinking. "Aren't you concerned," they ask, "that your reputation will be ruined? Aren't you afraid that your future relationship may be jeopardized?" The truth is that I have already passed the stage of being embarrassed, ashamed and humiliated. I have been to depths of emotional despair that the average person never even comes close to experiencing. I've experienced the darkness of soul. I've been a loser, an adulterer, a liar, a manipulator and most of all, a pretender. I've considered and attempted suicide because of depression, oppression and suppression, which is the need for my confession. Most of all, I don't believe that my life is my own; I believe that it belongs to you. Every step, every wrong move, every right move was for you to gather information that will help you to become a better person. It is not until this time that I have spent with you that I have felt liberated and truly free.

If you don't get anything else out of this book, I would hope that you received the fact that your life is not yours and that others need to hear your story, whether good, bad or indifferent. You are someone special. Remember, you can't continue to hide behind the mask of shame and embarrassment. This is what the enemy uses to defeat your purpose. And if you lose, then we all lose. Change starts from the inside out, not the other way around. Writing this book has been a truly remarkable experience. I have cried, I have smiled and laughed. I have come to grips with who I am. I've learned that who I am, is not necessarily who I am going to be, and that I will always be a work-in-progress, chasing perfection.

I've also accepted that I am capable of being the best person I can be without guilt or shame, and that I don't have to be captive in my own mind. I can still be the minister God called me to be, without the pulpit and deceitfulness, but with a real heart for His people. Ladies, I now realize that you are the queens of the earth and I have gained a newfound respect for you. I will always respect you for the beautiful creatures that you are.

I'm sure that most of you are expecting a happy ending, but unfortunately, that's not going to happen. My goal here was to tell the truth, and my integrity means everything. That is the path I am going to stay on. I have not yet worked through all of my issues. I am still sleeping around, sharing web cam sessions with women and still seeking attention. I still cry at night, longing to heal from the past, wondering if I will ever reach my full destiny. I will promise you that you can always count on me to be up front and honest with you. For now, I will continue to change the world, start-ing with me. Somewhere along the way, I don't quite remember when, I gave up my mask, in exchange for my purpose, and I hope that if you are a pretender, you will follow suit. If you are the victim of a pretender, I hope that you will begin to see beyond the mask. Take ownership of your life, of your destiny, of your emo-tions. It's not about me—it is all about you. That is why I decided to unveil the mask of the pretender.

THE POEM

    To all of the women that I've hurt, Manipulated
and deceived,

    For you that are still skeptical about me And still
don't believe.

    I understand the hurt

    And pain that I have caused,

    Which allows me to feel

    And to reminisce about my flaws

    You are the ultimate queens

    And it's important that I make that clear, Even
while I am writing this,

    From my face, drops a tear.

    To you, I am emotionally tied,

    Running from it, I tried.

    The necessity to surrender was necessary

    For it to be bonified.

    Please forgive me,

    For I am the symbol of imperfection:

    One who lost his way and veered off

    The road called The Right Direction.

    In my haste

    To become a winner,

It's important for me to say I have
repented,
And no longer am I a pretender.

REFLECTIONS

I am honored that you have joined me on my journey to transparency. Now, it is time for you to decide if this will just be another book you read, or if it will be the launching point for your own journey of self-discovery. Whether you are a Pretender, or find that you gravitate toward them in relationships, I invite you to begin the self-examination process that can be the first step towards your total freedom from the mask. The following questions are suitable for group discussions or private introspection. If you keep a journal, this might make a good entry. Consider each question carefully, and answer each one honestly. Also, add the questions "Why?" or "Why not?" after each, depending on whether you answer "yes" or "no".

Don't be afraid of the truth...it's the pretending that hurts in the end. Remember, if you are ever going to take off the mask, the first person who has to see you...is *you*.

QUESTIONS

1. Do you deny the truth when someone points it out to you?

2. Are you addicted to something that you haven't told anyone about?

3. Do you care about what people think about you?

4. Is life about you or others?

5. Do you manipulate and deceive to get your way?

6. Do you cheat on your spouse/significant other?

7. Can you relate to the incidents in this book?

8. Do you love yourself?

9. Are you a pretender?